Note from the author: I would love to see photos of you with your book! Where you're reading it, where it lives, your favourite poems...tag me in everything! @positivelysian

Making Sugar out of Life

Siân Williams

"Still, what I want in my life
is to be willing
to be dazzled -
to cast aside the weight of facts

and maybe even
to float a little
above this difficult world.
I want to believe I am looking

into the white fire of a great mystery.
I want to believe that the imperfections
are nothing -
that the light is everything..."

Mary Oliver, "The Ponds"

For my beautiful mum ~

who taught me to look for magic in unexpected places.

And a **special** thank you to my soul mate, Grant,
my *sol* mate, Georgia,
and the rest of the wolf pack -
your support, encouragement, love and divine energy
is such a blessing in my life.

I am so lucky to share this timeline with you all.

Contents

Preface

As I enter the last stretch of my twenties, I find myself in a perpetual state of psychological spring cleaning. The finality of this chapter, and the looming of a new one, satisfies the same part of my soul that loves to start a new notebook. It feels pregnant with potential. 'First day back at school with a load of new stationary' energy. I'm so looking forward to putting my best handwriting on a brand new page...my *thirties*.

This mentality is the by-product of a hard truth: one day I will be dead. I have always been unsettled by my eventual non-existence. In fact, I was five when I had my first panic attack about death. Specifically, how *long* I'll be dead for. Eternity is a bloody long time. But as morbid as it seems, from this great fear has come my greatest asset: I am forever chasing joy. Because if I am to be subject to such an inevitable fate, I best make the damn most of being alive.

It is both a blessing and a curse to be so aware that I only get one run at this. I want to savour and drown in it all, which often means my calendar sighs at the weight of its commitments and my bed groans when I roll in, yet again, past a sensible bedtime. Time is truly of the essence - this has never been lost on me - and I'm determined to design a wonderful life. I want to look back when I'm ninety nine (or however long we'll be living by then) and know that I really *milked* it.

Naturally, there are days when I don't feel quite so full of vigour, but I have learnt that both light and shade are necessary in creating depth; one cannot exist without the other. Breaking off my engagement and starting again, navigating the brutal minefield of modern dating, and falling deeply in love again, are just some of the themes in this book that affirm this.

Another theme largely at play in my mind, and therefore in my poems, is the inescapable tension and restriction one feels when recovering from an eating disorder. I am smothered by its presence, and yet, I believe to my core that life is to be lived, *fully*. I am pulled in opposite directions by freedom

1

and control. This see-saw between wanting to fit society's ceaseless and ever-changing standards vs. wanting to live deliciously, without guilt, is one I haven't quite learnt how to balance yet.

I am a work in progress - and I embrace the process. I try to picture life as a garden in which I can grow what I give my attention to. Of course, I'm only human, and occasionally, I'll let the garden spread into an impenetrable, dry, and spiky mass. Try as I might, I can never ignore the obvious truth for long: that the only person who can tend to the weeds is me.

But the weeds, the flowers, the light and the shade...they're all part of the cyclical nature of living. We are all our own projects of transformation. If our garden becomes a mess in certain seasons, we can pop our gloves on and go again. There is so much comfort to be found in this. And through it all, we must never forget that to *have* a garden, in whatever state, is a gift.

'Making Sugar out of Life' is a poetic journey through my life so far - an ongoing cycle of: pull weeds, plant seeds, bloom, and repeat. For this reason, the poems start a little heavier at the beginning - stick with it, I promise you can smell the flowers as you turn more pages.

If you take anything away from this book, let it be this: your garden is yours to design. And you only get **one** - for a limited time. So, enjoy the landscaping of it! Pull weeds when you need to. Plant only what brings you joy. Bloom in your entirety. Then, repeat.

1.

Pull weeds

The affair

I gave my innocence to a single bed
with Hello Kitty sheets
in September
It left a stain of cherry-red
on her Egyptian cotton
in October

A lesson;
never to ignore my screaming gut
or scarlet flags, thrashing
in 90mph Devonshire winds

I promised not to tell
their kids
via a 13p text
on a Nokia with a Betty Boop case, proof
of all the things I was not

**You are cordially invited
to the funeral of my wedding**

An ivory dress hangs on
the back of my spare room door
I need to sell it
give the money back to my mum
and nan - who thought I was mad
to buy the first dress I tried on
Maybe she saw
the life I wasn't destined for
Maybe I am

If they hadn't bought it I would burn it
Hold a funeral
for the life I didn't settle on
Scatter the ashes
in all the places I've felt most alive
since and hope
that trees made of lace
grow in every garden
of every woman
who finds herself wondering
if there's more

There is

Sending nudes

Lust feels like love
bites between legs
Nudes in hidden folders
that would make your mother Google 'exorcism'
Saying no to every sweet man
who wants to be more
than a stain
of aftershave on pillows
that you snort
like an addict

A life before blue eyes

They board up windows before storms
like you
but I would let you
suck
every door from its frame
rip the roof from my head
and feel grateful
to be part of the chaos
I would let you
shatter
every window I didn't board up
leave disaster in your wake
I would let you

Honey

You cannot blame the wasp
for the sting
if he has circled you
for the past 6 months
and you continued
to cover yourself
in honey

S.O.S.

If he feels like danger
send up an emergency flare
watch it fizzle out
and disappear
as
 quickly
   as
     it
     went
     up
     .

Learn from this.

The wrong size

I mostly keep you in the closet
with my other vintage dreams
that never did fit quite right
Beside the faded jeans
with ripped knees
I keep, hoping
one
day
they
might

The situationship

'Casual' ~ a word
for low to no effort, a lack
of passion, longevity
bedding me
and I know it's 2022
and we're all swiping right
and there's 500 girls at your fingertips, but
keep it magic or stop
wasting my time
I am here for a flash ~
a shooting star
on the timeline of eternity
and there is not one atom in me
that vibrates at the frequency
of keeping it casual, okay?

If I'm still single when I'm fifty

My heart is safe among pretty sleeves
Black discs and lyric sheets
Devotion without jealousy
Nostalgia, memories, melodies
If I'm still single when I'm fifty
I'll marry my record player

Starving

Be the woman in the red swimsuit
eat cereal twice a day (30g), don't complain
that you're starving
drink a pint of water
trick your body
have a coffee
remember, sugar is a sin
suck it in
be feminine
be soft
be Marilyn Monroe
but pull your towel around your stomach
if it folds when you sit
just tone up
like Kim. Big bums are a win
but ignore what I said about Marilyn
heroine chic is back in
cut your meals to one a day, don't complain
that you're starving
drink green tea
confident is the sexiest thing you can be
and have fun
have another glass
order dessert, oh don't be boring
why are you so miserable?
lighten up
you're the woman in the red swimsuit

Shouting into the afterlife

Today I wore my great nan's ring
I never wear gold
but this is an emergency

I am convinced
that she is wearing it
in some dimension next door
separated by a curtain of stardust
or whatever the universe makes
its borders from

I begged her
walk beside me, fingers entwined
guide me
I am desperate!
From the depths of time, deliver me
a great big fucking slap

Truly, I am exhausted
from carrying the devil
on my back, I need you
to shake me,
break me open and write it on my brain
that one day I won't count
the inches on my arms,
I will simply pray that they are strong
enough to lift my grandchildren,
strong enough
to tend to the blossoms
of my life

If you can hear me, turn
your head in dismay, say
I am ungrateful and ridiculous
for feeling this
grotesque when I have everything
to feel blessed about

Are you there?
I am sorry, I know
you are resting but I will twist
this ring around my finger until it stirs
you from wherever you are
This is an emergency

I am an imposter

This poem comes to you
from Nice, France, where I am
an imposter
and everyone is beautiful
and slim and strings
of diamantés cling
to toned, gold stomachs

I'm on the beach
trying to look normal, wondering
how their organs fit
in such tiny spaces
The baguette on every table here
must be for the men

I am making notes
to cut
portion sizes next week,
start running, start
moulding next Summer
into something less soft

With every "au revoir" I caveat that I will
be back and fit
right in next summer

Toying with death on a monthly basis

Sorry, I can't come into the office today
I don't feel well. My uterus is screaming /
I am being tortured from the inside /
There is a fishing hook in my lower back
being pulled by the moon / I need to lay in
the fetal position / My stomach is so swollen
it hurts to carry / My clothes don't fit /
I'm two dress sizes bigger and I'm sick
of myself / Everything is wrong /
There is a tiny thing playing the drums
on my temples / My knees
are throbbing / I am doubting my entire existence /
I need to wear my old knickers, I can't go
2 hours without bleeding
on something / I don't want anyone to see me
like this - I will blow
out every candle
I come into proximity with / I will infect you
with this feeling. Go away

I don't want to die

The first time it came I was five
arrives in the night / on the morning commute
as I tuck an umbrella beside sodden boots
as I squeeze a tea bag
for a third time. It creeps
on the outskirts of a beautiful day
threatens to stay - stains
a bruise of red wine on tipsy lips, rips
the edges of my favourite book, took
my favourite white top and dyed it
grey - clutters the space
like the laundry that never dries
don't cry
you're ok, you're ok, you're ok

A grave I won't visit

There are two women buried in the walls
of a maisonette in Zone 6
5 coats of magnolia to cover the red
splash on the ceiling
Strange, grey mermaids
under the bathroom tiles
The impression of a saucepan
on the kitchen wall -
doubled as a weapon
Recurring nightmares
of a wolf at the door

On their last day, there was a single mattress,
a record player, "Miracle Aligner" on repeat
And it was a miracle - *is* a miracle
that we are here and they are there
and we were them

I flinch every time I hear your name

With every finger that clasped
my mother's throat
my vertebrae turned
to tungsten and then some
soft, young edges leaked
the safety I had known,
transformed it
into metal and I was always
going to have to weld it
into art or
become hard

Pretending I know what I'm doing

I am pretending I know what I'm doing when all I want to do is paint /
sit by a lake / contemplate / pray. Responsibility is growing vines across
my back with no end date on the contract. I'm losing sleep over finance
trackers and somewhere someone is washing an old tin mug in a
waterfall. I'm entering formulas to formulate an income and when I die
they'll formulate how much tax I owe and my loved ones will formulate
the cost of the coffin and the buffet and I wonder when did life become
about formulas and not about lying in nature at every opportunity?
The weight of it is silly when you think of the outcome we are all
stumbling towards and I'm sorry to remind you of our collective
mortality but that spreadsheet doesn't seem so important now does it?

2.

Plant seeds

The relief of the light

Maybe one day I will
build a house of soil and dew drops, grow
my arms towards the sun and drip
rain from the tips of my fingers
I'll count rings instead of wrinkles
Hug infant seeds
between my toes ~ teach them
the dark precedes the relief
of the light
Tuck them in
Do yoga with the wind
Feel the droplets edge
back up my spine, give thanks
to the dandelions
for granting wishes
to the seeds and kiss them
to sleep

Wild thing

I was nudged awake by whiskers
pushed the love away, resisted
morning
Sent a flare up for coffee -
a mountain scoop
Prayed it would save me
from a night spent howling
at the moon
Gulped it like a wild thing
Lit the candle by my bed - an offering
Watched the flame, honoured
the many fires I've danced around
in previous lives
Felt the coffee beans roll
vitality to my sleeping limbs
The air smells like sugar
and I am alive

Be the change

Us Londoners have learnt to brace
and ignore the tourists
jolting dramatically
as the tube moves off
Just like we have learnt
to ignore personal space
and politeness
to sit in silence
forget kindness
And whilst we might offer our seats
to the elderly and the women
growing humans
We pretend we are not
human and stare, idly
past the beggar,
the drunk and the broken, please
tell me I am not the only one left
who can see
these spaces that take
and dim our light
are where we must shine
them the brightest???

Leave a message

Sorry, I can't come to the phone right now, I am too busy
mentally debating whether to have another coffee /
topping up my liquid eyeliner / starting projects and never finishing
them / touching the bark of every tree I walk past / wondering
what I'll regret not doing when I'm old / hoping I get to grow old /
complaining about feeling bloated / sucking my stomach in / worrying
about the calories in hazelnut syrup /and everything / avoiding cleaning
the oven / wondering how many hours of my life I'll spend cleaning /
being overwhelmed at all the WhatsApp messages I haven't replied to /
scrolling social media / wondering if I should delete social media /
buying another plastic bag from Asda / marvelling at the bluest sky /
listening
for guidance / panicking about my mortality /
thinking about how I'm just a vessel for my soul / still wishing
I was thinner / dancing in my granny pants / living vibrantly, please
leave a message after the tone

I feel

I feel like someone replaced my frontal lobe with a tea towel /
like I exist in this world but at arm's length from everything in it /
like I'm constantly seeking but I don't know what I'm looking for / I feel
unheard / unexpressed / overlooked / beaten down / exhausted
on every level, in every way / I'm in the meeting place
between content and inconsolable / torn between two worlds -
the one I thought I needed and the one that wants me / I feel trapped
distracted / empty / like no matter what I do, it is never enough /
My voice is blanketed by your ego but don't be fooled by my quiet resolve
I am strength internalised / I am destined for more / I am terrified
but I'm trusting the universe and its plan for me / I am
on the precipice of something great / I am limitless

I posted a link on my Instagram where people could respond anonymously
to the prompt 'I feel'. This is a collaborative poem made from the answers I
received. I am deeply thankful for those who took part, for trusting me with
their vulnerability and allowing me to document such a prominent
collection of human emotions.

Time you won't get back

A
grain
of
sand
falls
as you double tap a red heart
on someone else's adventure /
someone else's lunch /
someone else's cat
completing an assault course

A
grain
of
sand
falls
as you double tap a red heart
on someone else's sunset
someone else's new dress /
someone else's boomerang
of 4 clinking glasses

34 grains
of sand
just fell
as
you
read
this
poem

A ticking clock

Tell me, is it lust
or ovulation?
Hunger
or the longing of a body, ripe
with evolutionary responsibility?
Does my body want
you
or do I?

You can do better

Stop dirtying your knees
for someone who couldn't care
less about your unsettled heart
Giving yourself in measures
that would paint red
on the cheeks of your ancestors
Whipping up your own waters
into rapids and then wondering
why you ache
from swimming against the tide

My dear, get over your shallow lust
Push him off that bloody pedestal
Those who cannot see your light
(even as they are drenched in it!)
will forever be blind

For you

Imagine being given a gift so rare
it is the only one of its kind to exist
in all of eternity ————— infinite
numbers of cells and systems
one hundred million
devoted neurons jumping
for you
across synapses delivering
one hundred million
messages past lungs expanding
and blood pumping
and tiny hairs springing up
to cuddle the sensitive parts of you
for you
one hundred million
moments of synchronicity and luck
the codes of your ancestors
twirling in unison
for you for you for you
Imagine!!!!!!

Just imagine
unwrapping the inconceivable gift of it
and responding
with one hundred million
thoughts of disapproval

Sewing joy

Did you know
that you can hand-pick
all of your favourite feelings
like flowers -
arrange your life
so that there is a bouquet
on every table?

That you can sew joy
into your mornings
your lunch hours / your life
by choosing
your favourite colours
and following the threads -
simply grateful
you have a needle
to sew with?

Leaving a trail

If your fingerprints stained everything
you touched
and your words materialised
leaving a trail
you would choose wisely

If you could see your imprint
colouring the world
you would paint yourself differently
embodying the finest china
set kept for best
you would move delicately

Your fingerprints
decorating
the plump flesh of the mango you turned
in your gifted hands and put back /
the book your best friend is reading
before bed because you told her to /
the brain of a colleague
who repeats your advice to his wife
over breakfast / the shells
you thumbed and put back to sea

You are leaving marks on the world

are you choosing wisely?

A poetic poke in the ribs

I wish I could write a metaphor that hasn't already been written.
A jab of a metaphor that would poke you in the ribs. A sinking
feeling of a metaphor. A hard truth.
What string of words would it take
for you to start living?
To start dancing instead of stumbling?
To move with vigour - not toleration?
Will it take someone to die for you to realise? That one day
it'll be your name engraved in the stone?
That you only get one?

3.
Bloom

Making sugar out of life

If you ever find yourself disenchanted with life, remember: your plants turn sunlight into sugar whilst you sleep. The soil beneath your feet is alive and affirming: you can uproot whenever you need to. Equally, wiggle your toes where you stand and be planted anew. Water climbs the stem of the bathroom orchid as you shower. It will bloom orange on a melancholy Wednesday as if it knew.

Right now, at every point where Earth meets mystery, the sea is teasing the sand. The sun leaves stains on reckless shoulders. A squirrel hugs an acorn to its chest, planning ahead. An elderly pair are falling in love over tea at their local library. A brilliant pink sky dyes the inside of a train carriage.

Someone in dungarees is firing teacups in a kiln that will eventually sit on your best friend's table. She will make tea and eat strawberries from the punnet whilst you unfold. You will put yourself back together in her kitchen and leave fuller. The Earth will massage your heels on the walk home.

Learn from your plants. Look to the sun. Hold green solar panels to the sky. They are always making sugar out of life. If you find yourself disenchanted, remember.

I freckle my cheeks with gold

My nails are red for a reason
My eyes lined Cleopatra black
I wear sparkles and feathers,
silver rings on my toes
Sometimes,
I freckle my cheeks with gold
I am the endless canvas
A work of art
A collage of everything
I've ever ached for

A gift.

I decorate my body
to celebrate
the marvel that she is

You decorate the space

Next time you upload
a selfie and count the likes, remember
that once you were nothing
a void
and now you
decorate the space
with laughter
and mischief and the sun
turns
your eyes an unusual
delicious hue
of Autumn
and pretty plants grow
because you water them
and that should be enough

The eighth wonder

I wonder why
we have named all the wonders
of the world and haven't yet thought
to name ourselves

Cowboy boots

There are much more interesting parts to me
than my cowboy boots
and where I bought them
I would rather tell you that
I have my scuba diving qualification
That I once saw God in a sunset
in Whitstable
That some of my soul is still sitting
on a bridge in Saint-Sauveur
tearing at a pain au raisin

I would rather tell you
that I erase all of my artistic mistakes
using cotton buds
which feels like cheating
and I used to write to 3 fairies, you know
I never really stopped
believing in magic
I cast my own spells sometimes
in the form of gratitude lists
and firm hugs
and in baking crumble
for my old neighbour
but yes, they are great boots. Thank you
for the compliment

To the girls with pumpkin decor

Maybe Autumn feels so full of magic
because we were told
that pumpkins grow into carriages

That they would carry us
in pastel gowns
to men with promises as big as castles

But the fairytales are outdated
and I am writing my own -
being my own fairy godmother
blending pumpkins into soup
driving myself on midnight adventures

creating my own alchemy.

When I want to feel mysterious

Slice the pink cushion of my brain
and you will find cats
asleep in all the nooks and crannies, hundreds
of books organised by colour,
old pop-punk posters on the walls and
enough disco balls to illuminate
the expanding black

Every lyric I've ever heard might pour
onto your shoes, carry you
down a lazy river alive with frogs
from my Grandad's old pond on Kings Road

You'll drift
past a mystical garden
where fairies live
I leave them tiny pieces of bubblegum
to say thank you
for sprinkling magic on my life

I go there sometimes
to undress
and drape myself in ivy
when I want to feel
mysterious

Where do you go?

Gentle hands

They say the universe repeats
lessons until you learn them
and I was perpetually receiving
lessons on lessons and yet
never learning
that the flash in your gut is never wrong
that the word 'casual' means never
and that 'it's not you, it's me'
means it's you

But now,
I'm walking home
in the rain and the light
turns spilled oil into magic,
and there's a man asleep in his bed
holding my heart
with the same delicacy one adopts
wandering rows of antiques,
tucking in careful elbows,
making sure not to break anything

Mystery man

He looks at me like I look at the moon
Loves me through all
my phases
Even the ones where I am more wolf
than twinkling star or planet

Perhaps because he is more
a cosmic wonder than anything
I have ever found
in a textbook
or night sky -

More enigma than man,
created with a precision
that makes pyramids blush
and as much a mystery,
with a true north pointing
directly to me

I've been waiting this whole time

Being loved by you feels like a Saturday
in 22 degrees / pressing lavender
to my nose / like lying on a lilo
with my hand half in the water / delicious
and deliberate / like la passeggiata /
an act of worship /
in which we are both the offering and the alter / sacred
surrender / like downing tools / being
in flow / like poetry / the beginning
and the end of everything / like I've been waiting
this whole time

Happy wrinkles

If we manage to set the world on fire,
the clouds browning
at the edges like old maps
I will ache for the world
it's cats and museums,
the stories, stalactites,
libraries and love letters,
unfinished embroidery hoops
and songs half-scribbled,
that will be sucked into some black
hole somewhere, but mostly
I will ache for more time
being the cause
of the happy wrinkles
at the sides of those eyes

My best friend just paid for her full astrological chart

She swears
life unfolds at the mercy of the moon

That today is predetermined
by the coordinates of Saturn,
her time of birth,
and her Virgo rising

I do not need to check her astrology to know
that she is made of stars
and the answers have been inside her
all along

Curfews

I will struggle to punish my children
for getting home past some made-up curfew
for oozing the sickly perfume of neon
alcopops and tobacco.
All of the times I've felt most alive
have been in the space between bending the rules
and burying them alive. Like missing the last train
because I was slurring on a balcony overlooking Big Ben,
licking rum off the tongue of a guitarist
from my favourite band and napping
on a bench in Victoria Station, giddy
on guitar strings.
I have dipped my torso in a lake
with a belly full of mushrooms, next to a 'no swimming' sign,
engulfed in a sparkly feeling
that I am the entire solar system and more. I have broken
into a deserted Chinese restaurant and danced
until 4am, to music that made my ribs rattle -
and even though someone tried to strangle me
in the toilets lit by tea lights,
it is a hilarious story to tell over dinner.

Of course,
when the rebel I have created returns home,
1 hour late, or more
I will turn my face into something disapproving,
threaten their luxuries, teach them
about consequences but underneath
my stern exterior, child
know that I am cheering you on
and I can't wait to hear the stories
you are writing.

In celebration of the senses

I am living life the same way I eat a creme egg:
eagerly, messily, all tongue.
Greedily
sucking my lips
at the cruel deliciousness of it.
Simultaneously seduced and the seducer. Dancing
in celebration of the senses, yet
never quite satisfied,
never quite full,
never quite ready for the end

Skimming stones

Sometimes I forget
that I am energy and I am creating
the experience around me
That what I hold onto
multiplies, makes neural pathways
and becomes my day-to-day
I am choosing my destiny every second -
every decision
is weaving the next story but
I am not always conscious of this.
Sometimes I forget
that a masterpiece needs to be crafted
This is not a journey that can be put on autopilot
I cannot throw a stone in the general direction
of the lake and hope
it will skim effortlessly,
in a perfect dance. I must always be aiming,
choosing, re-adjusting. Energy is malleable
and starts in the core of us
but it is easy to start a fire and forget
to stoke it, burying it in a list
of to-dos, falling
into a sleepwalk. When you feel the biting
cold is when you realise -
you have let the fire die out
But you are always only one thought
away from the next
spark

Where to sprinkle my ashes

in The Cavern / along Route des Peyrières / that square in Bergerac
where they do outdoor salsa classes / underneath the disco ball
at The Glade, mixed with glitter / somewhere you can always smell
fresh pastries and coffee beans

bury me amid the keys of a piano playing Canon in D / in the twirling cave
of a conch shell / in sea foam / in his pocket / in my mum's soft hair /
in my brother's clenching, newborn palm / in the forest by Capilano Bridge
in Vancouver / in the folds of the fells / between my cat's ears
wherever there is always thick, salty chips

Instructions for when I die

I might be dead when you are reading this. And not in a morbid way - just in the way that this book will most likely outlive me. If I am a dead poet, dear reader, know that right now as I write this, I am very much alive. In fact, I'm twenty nine, so I still have many books to write. And hangovers to endure. And countries to visit. And Christmas lights to untangle.

It's Saturday 4th November 2023 and I am the opposite of dead. I am fizzing with love. For a beautiful man, spectacular friends, music, picnics, coffee, the sea. With being alive and walking among the trees. With getting my hands dirty in antique shops. With glittery clothes, halloween, frogs, biscuits, and every song that has ever made the hairs stand up on my arms. I am so genuinely grateful to be here.

If I am a dead poet, please take this book on a walk in the woods. Place me where the sun makes patterns on the soil. Give my poems to the trees. Take me to a jumble sale. Buy something old that sparkles. Go to a café and leave me amongst the tea rings. Or take me home, open a bottle of red and dress mysteriously. Celebrate.

I realise I am asking quite a lot of you already, dear reader, but I have one more request. Every day, do something to send joy out into our world ~ she is giving, giving, and we must give back. Surprise someone. Vow to live life making kind ripples. Think of me. If joy is my legacy, I'll be a very happy dead poet.

About the author

Siân is an audio producer, painter and
poet, living in Rochester, England.
She would describe herself as a
woodland walk / charity shop / disco
ball / music / sunshine / poetry / life
enthusiast!

Growing up in music venues with her
DJ mum, and grandparents passionate
about 70's rock, music vibrates in her atoms. She studied Audio
Production at the University of Sussex and has spent her career so far
telling stories with sound. She fell in love with poetry in the Winter of
2022, during a writing course at her local bookshop; she sees now that all
great lyrics are poetry.

'Making Sugar out of Life' is her debut collection of poems. She dreams of
one day writing a self help book that inspires people to live boldly.

Printed in Great Britain
by Amazon